SHE'S **KILLIN'** IT

This Journal Belongs to:

SHE'S **KILLIN'** IT

Dedication

To my babe, Brennan, for continuing to light me up when I need it most; to Karina for keeping me grounded and sane; to my entire team for protecting and loving my baby as if it were their own; to my parents for their unconditional support; and to my Manifestation Babes for making everything possible. I love you guys.

Disclaimer

All information and resources found in this book are based on the opinions of the author, Kathrin Zenkina, owner of the Manifestation Babe Brand. All information is intended to motivate readers to make their own health care decisions after consulting with their healthcare provider. Kathrin Zenkina is nor a doctor, lawyer, psychiatrist, therapist and no part of this book shall be interpreted as a diagnosis for any medical condition. The information in this book is not intended to replace a one-on-one relationship with a qualified health care professional and is not intended as medical advice.

Copyright

INTRODUCTION

The Anxiety Attack That Changed My Life.

My journal saved me from one of my darkest places.

It was January 1st, 2016 when I experienced my very first anxiety attack. If you've ever had an attack before in your life, you know the kind of nightmare situation I am talking about. I'll never forget the feeling of what it felt like to *totally* lose control of my body, and allow panic, mixed with utter dread, overcome my body like a racing black cloud.

Like many other women out there, anxiety has always been something I just, you know, had to deal with. But this day was different. This day felt like all of my anxiety finally had enough of being repressed down. It wanted to escape like steam out of a boiling tea kettle with a tight spout.

Constant worry, stress, frustration, and doubt were emotions I felt on a daily basis. Being an empath and not knowing it, didn't help me very much either. Not only would I have to deal with my own shit, but apparently, I often processed others' shit too. If you're like me, you know exactly what I'm talking about.

So, when I finally found myself $25,000 in debt, broke, pumping my gas in $5 increments, miserable, and scared of where I was at in my life, I *really* began to experience some of my darkest moments. But none of them compared to this one. I'll never forget that New Years' Day

In the midst of panic, while feeling like my life was completely falling apart, my eyes immediately darted to a journal I had sitting on my desk. It was a journal given to me by my best friend, Stephanie, as a place to collect my thoughts and desires. I had it for a few months by then and never even opened it. I was never the type to write things in journals. In fact, I *tried* to keep a diary my entire childhood and the results were laughable. Each new diary would have 2 entries and then a 2-year gap between the entries.

Out of nowhere, I heard a voice say to me loud and clear: "Go out in nature, open this journal, and let it all out. You will figure it out when you do." I was so jolted by its intensity that I didn't have the guts to argue with it.

I followed my crystal-clear instructions and got into my 2012 white Volkswagen Jetta with a gas tank almost at E. The only place in nature that came to my mind was the back of Fox Island—an island about 2 miles from my parents' house. It had an incredible dock I would often visit in my high school days. It was a dock that had one of the most incredible views of Tacoma, Washington across the water. Every time I went there, I would never run into any people. It sounded like a great place to be mid-anxiety attack.

Arriving at the dock on the very back of the island, I drove into the lot, parked my car, took a deep breath and walked down the 25-30 steps leading down the hill onto the dock. I approached one of the few benches and sat down. My butt was instantly drenched from the rain that had just recently poured down. If you know anything about the Tacoma/Seattle area in Washington state, you'd know that everything is *always* wet. In this moment, I didn't care if I was soaked or dry. I couldn't feel my body except for an extremely tight ball in my throat and a heaviness on my chest. I opened the blank journal, picked up my pen and just started writing. I probably wrote for 2 hours straight.

I wrote about *everything.* Everything that bugged me, frustrated me, infuriated me, angered me, worried me, scared the hell out of me. Every single thought that rushed through my mind, I let it out on the paper. My deepest darkest thoughts. My biggest dreams and why I felt unworthy of them. How I thought that I was destined to be a failure. All the reasons why I didn't love myself. All of my frustrations about my finances. I. Let. It. All. Out.

Ten full written pages later, I noticed my handwriting started to change. I began to write slower, bolder, and bigger. In huge letters, the following words came onto my page:

"Kathrin, it's time you start to focus on abundance. Abundance, abundance, abundance. It is all around you. You are so extremely well taken care of, and you allow the littlest things to get in your way. You get in your own way. Focus on abundance. Abundance is your birthright. You are so divinely loved, guided, and protected. Use your tools to let out anything that isn't serving you, but don't be led to believe that this isn't an illusion. Your anxiety isn't real. It's an illusion. Use your journal to heal yourself. Start writing to let it all out. Start writing to organize your thoughts. Go back to your journal when you need it. And just wait to see what's waiting for you on the other side of this."

I had chills by the end of it. Where did this come from? But better yet, does it even matter? I felt so much BETTER. I felt an overwhelming sense of relief. Oh my God, did I feel like I could breathe again. I felt like there was a light at the end of the tunnel. Even though nothing actually changed in my life in that moment, I felt like I had a sense of control again, regardless of my current situation.

It's funny, looking back now. Journaling is part of my daily practice when it comes to self-growth, self-exploration, and personal development. Back then, I was always the girl who rolled her eyes at other people's journals. You know what I thought was meant by "journaling?" I would always picture a little girl writing about her entire day in a book starting the entry with "dear diary." I could never figure out the point of such an activity. I tried it myself so many times, and it never resonated with me. Besides, my hands *hurt* from handwriting. I'm way more of a typer. *Are you kidding me?*

That New Years' Day all of it changed.

I became an avid daily journaler after that day. I started to let out my frustrations long before they could manifest into anxiety. My journal became a safe space to communicate with the Universe. I used it as a powerful way to communicate with my higher self. Journaling was a means of getting to know myself better. To get to know the *real, raw* me better. I used it as a safe place to explore my desires, what I was manifesting on a daily basis, and a place to keep track of my goals. It very quickly become my favorite part of the day. I looked forward to the time periods set aside in my day to write in my journal.

My journal literally saved my life.

And that, my beautiful friend, is my story. I am so glad you picked up this 21-day journal to help you not only explore yourself and get to know your deepest desires, but also create your life into the very version that you've always envisioned it to be. I created this journal to help you manifest your kickass life.

Today, I work with thousands of women as a master mindset coach and success strategist. Helping women unleash their inner magic, break through their limitations, and manifest realities wilder than their wildest dreams is not only my greatest passion, but also my greatest gift. I feel like everything I've been through led me to this career path, and I couldn't be more grateful for it.

My number one goal with this journal is to stretch you. This isn't a place to just doodle, giggle, and write a couple of words down. This is a place where you will not only get to explore some transformative prompts, but also goal set, keep track of your progress, figure out what you need to do in order to keep growing into the best version of yourself, and get in touch with your subconscious mind.

I strongly believe that the biggest key to my personal success has been the fact that I stopped allowing my conscious mind to rule my life, my decisions, and my emotions. Instead, I decided to employ my subconscious mind on a fulltime basis, and I haven't looked back. Letting go of overthinking and overanalyzing has not only served me well, but it cut down my anxiety levels to an enormous degree.

Our subconscious minds are incredible. It's the part of our mind that holds all of our secrets to success. Our subconscious minds hold the answers to every single question we could ever ask about literally anything. Our subconscious minds know how to take us from where we are now to where we want to go. It also knows the easiest, simplest, and most straightforward path to our dream life. Sounds like an amazing thing, right? Our only problem is that we don't utilize it enough. Not even close to its max potential. It's there to serve us, but we keep shutting it down. We constantly get in our own way by consciously overanalyzing and overthinking everything, when we can just get into our subconscious flow.

This journal is going to help you tap into your subconscious mind. As you'll soon find when you start the 21-day journey, I ask that you not over think any of the entries. Go with your gut the entire way. Begin with the very first thing that comes to mind. This is because the subconscious mind doesn't need any time to think. The subconscious mind knows the truth and the right answer as soon as you ask it. The answer comes instantly. You'll find that you'll end up surprising yourself on every single page that you work through. It's going to be an amazing journey of self-discovery.

In just a moment I am going to explain to you everything that you can expect from this journal, and how to approach each section that you will come across. But before I do, I want to mention one more thing: Make the *commitment* to find the time every single morning and every single evening to work through your journal. This journal was created with prompts in mind to help you go deep within. Prompts that will elevate your life to the next level if you give them some time. Questions that will cause you to explore the depths of your soul. Sections that will help you become a master manifestor and a true creator of your own destiny.

You've come to the right place if you are someone who is ready to drop the bullshit and create her kickass life. You were meant for so much more, gorgeous, and I know you know this too. You wouldn't have crossed paths with this journal if it weren't true.

HOW THE JOURNAL *Works*

Every single day of the journal will have many consistencies with a few differences. The daily inspirational quote, morning journal prompt, and morning mantra will differ and depend on a different theme for each day. The journal is split up into sections that are meant to be filled out every single morning, and sections that are meant to be filled out every single evening. Each section should take no longer than 20 minutes per morning (including a 5-minute meditation) and 15 minutes per evening. Remember, we are working with our subconscious minds here. There is no need to overthink the process. Focus on the very first thoughts that come to mind and just *write*. If you've ever heard of the phrase "automatic writing," this is what we're going for here. Even if you aren't entirely sure how to answer something, pretend you know. See what comes out of that fun space of pretending.

This journal journey is unlike any other because not only will you learn a ton about yourself, you will also learn to set goals, track progress, and reflect on how to improve yourself on a daily basis. This is the ultimate self-improvement journal to truly tap into your ability to create or manifest your life to be exactly as you want it.

Gratitude:

If gratitude isn't already a part of your daily life, prepare for some major shifts to occur in your happiness levels, fulfillment, and overall energy. One thing that has dramatically changed my life over the last year is starting every single morning reflecting on at least 5 things I am grateful for in my life.

One of the highest vibration emotions that exists in the universe is gratitude. What we appreciate, feel grateful for, and send unconditional love to, flourishes in our lives. Just like what we focus on expands, what we feel grateful for shows up even more. If you want more of *anything* in your life, you must first feel grateful for what you already have. Through abundance, more abundance is created.

Goal Setting & Accomplishments:

Part of killin' it in life is to stay focused on what you *want* versus what you *don't want.* Where most people go wrong in manifesting their kickass lives is that they focus way more on all the things that they *don't* want, and hardly ever know what they *do* want. They end up manifesting more of what they don't want and drive themselves crazy wondering why that is.

Although there are prompts in this journal to help you work on some things from the past, the rest of the sections are meant to keep you focused on the future. What do you intend to accomplish that day? What was your progress that day? What is your 21-day goal? And what is your daily progress toward that goal?

At the end of the introduction section of the journal, right before we go into the meat of the content, you will find a quick goal setting workshop to help you set a goal for yourself for the next 21 days. The reason why we want to set a goal is because I want to help you blow your own mind as to how far you truly can come in life in just a single month. Change doesn't have to take *years* as so many of us are led to believe. Major changes can happen in as little as 21 days as long as you put the focus, intention and action into the right direction.

Desires:

Something else that we don't do enough of in this enormous, unlimited, unbelievably amazing Universe is ask for more of what we want. We, especially as women, are so afraid of dreaming. We are afraid of asking for more because we think that we must be self-sacrificial and be grateful for having just enough. Although it's great and all to be grateful for what we already have, as that's super important, we don't ever want to settle. Life isn't about settling.

We live in an unlimited Universe that's forever expanding. It's actually part of our programming to have desires, wants and wishes for our lives. Our souls are trying to expand *with* the Universe and what most of us end up doing is going against the grain. We are literally swimming against the current when we deny ourselves what we want.

There is no limit as to what we can manifest or create in our lives. Yet, we go around pretending like there is some limit set up for us. We see ourselves as living in a zero-sum world where we think that if we have more, someone else will have less. Or if someone else has more, we will end up having less. That's just not how the Universe actually works. This kind of thinking literally goes against spiritual laws.

We live on an abundant planet where there is plenty go to around and we can literally be, do, and have whatever we may wish. So, part of this journal is to get you comfortable with that. Something I did right at the beginning of my daily journaling journey was to create two lists every single morning. One for what I'm grateful for that morning, and one for what I desire to manifest into my life that day. No guilt, no shame, no ill feelings involved. I kept reminding myself that desires are part of being a human being. The Universe is on a constant mission to bless us, and the last thing we want to do is say, "no thank you, I'd rather suffer."

Part of working *with* the Universe rather than working against it is to get really good at just that – asking for what you want. You'll see that I will get you into this practice on a daily basis. Just make sure you dream really big. The world is your oyster!

Intentions:

What's the difference between goal setting and setting intentions? Goal setting is creating an outcome to focus on and work towards for a specified amount of time until it is accomplished.

Example: It is now (insert date here) and I have earned $100,000 in my online business.

Setting an intention is creating a statement or objective to live by. It is focused more on the present moment and helps keep you in touch with your goal.

Example: I intend to be more mindful, focus on the present moment, and remind myself that the money will continue to flow my way on a continuous basis whether I am putting in the hours or not.

You will see that intention setting is a daily practice in this journal aside from focusing on your overall 21-day goal. I set goals and intentions simultaneously and they almost always go hand in hand for me. One is my outcome, and one is how I choose to live that day so that I can get one step closer to my outcome.

Letting it Out:

As I mentioned earlier, part of my struggle before I started to journal on a regular basis was that I would suffer from anxiety almost daily. This was mainly because I was repressing my negative emotions. I would struggle and strive to keep down any stress, worry, or frustration that I would come across in my day-to-day life. If something happened, I refused to address it. I would either ignore it or stuff it deep down inside of me and try to hold it down using a metaphorical lid. This repression was the reason why I had that major anxiety attack. The reason why I ended up feeling so much better is because my journal allowed me to finally take the lid off and blow off some steam.

You'll find in both the morning and evening sections that there is a very safe space for you to let out anything that is bothering you. Any thought processes that you *know* are going to affect you that day, this is the place you want to write them down. You don't have to actually solve your problems to feel the relief that writing them down can bring you. Just getting them *out* of you and onto paper allows your mind to relax. It allows your mind to know that if it did choose to come back and process those thoughts at a later time, they are written on paper.

Keep in mind that these sections in particular don't need to be filled every single day. They are optional. If you truly have nothing bothering you, no need to come up with issues. We want to keep you in a positive, high vibration place for all 21 days. Just know that this is the place to deal with any negativity if it does happen to come up – both morning and evening.

Meditation:

There are thousands of benefits to meditation, but one that has always been my favorite, and will continue to be my favorite, is the incredible inspiration and guidance that comes through silence and stillness.

Just like I used to think journaling was silly at first, I thought meditation was equally as silly. Being a master implementer and the queen of productivity, sitting still has always been an impossible task. If I wasn't being productive or working on something constantly, I would feel incomplete. Meditation had always looked to me like the biggest waste of time. How in the hell can you be productive by sitting there, legs crossed, palms up, breathing deeply with your *eyes closed?!* It made zero sense to me.

Until, of course, I actually tried it.

If it wasn't for my willingness to start meditating, I wouldn't be nearly as inspired nor connected to the Universe as I am today. When we pray, we are asking. When we are meditating, we are listening to the answers to our prayers. They go hand in hand and you can't really have one without the other.

On this 21-day journey, I want you to start meditating. If you don't already, you'll soon find that just 5 minutes per day in the mornings is all you need. Just to practice quieting your mind and listening. To help you out, I have created a 5-minute guided meditation which can be found by visiting: manifestationbabe.com/sheskillinitmeditation.

Push play when it's time to meditate, close your eyes, and allow me to take care of the rest.

Mantra:

I strongly believe that affirmation and mantra work has been one of my superpowers when it comes to manifesting my desires.

Each morning before you start the day, I will leave you with a daily mantra. The purpose for this mantra is to first, read it; Then, say it out loud 5 times; And, last, take it with you throughout the day. Do your best to repeat it as often as you can consciously remember to, and see how you feel by the end of the day.

I kid you not, every single mantra that I have ever created for myself and got in the practice of repeating to myself throughout the day, has manifested into my reality. This is because our subconscious minds listen to every single thing we say out loud. The subconscious mind is like a bridge between us and the Universe. Whatever is absorbed into the subconscious is what you'll see manifested in your reality.

Not only that, but the best way to reprogram your subconscious mind is through daily repetition. Thus, repeating the mantras at a minimum of 5 times every single morning. Using repetition plus speaking your mantras out loud will literally change your life. Don't believe me? Just try it for the next 21 days. You'll be blown away!

HOW TO GOAL SET PROPERLY: *The Mini Pre-Journal Training*

Before I let you go on your epic journey of inspiration, self-growth, and personal development, I want to make sure we have a goal set up for you for the next 21 days. Not just any goal, but one that is achievable, fun to work toward, compelling and means something to you.

Did you know that simply by writing down your goal on paper you're something like 50% more likely to achieve it? Just by writing it down! Imagine what happens when you not only write it down every single day, but also break down how exactly you will achieve that goal. Tracking your daily progress takes it even further. With that many reminders, how much easier would it be for you to take action on the things that matter to you most?

However, first we need to know how to *properly* set a goal. It amazes me that no matter how many clients I work with or workshops I host, I will *always* come across at least several people who either never set a goal before or don't even know where to start. And if these women have set goals before, it never ceases to amaze me how vague and uninspiring they are! Like what in the world does it mean to "have more money?"

The problem with vague goal setting is that your subconscious mind is extremely lazy. Not lazy in the bad sense, but lazy in the sense that it is always going to take the path of least resistance to bring you want you want conserving the most energy in the meantime. When you set a goal like "I want more money," your subconscious mind will take you in the literal sense. You will walk by your living room in the morning one day, see a penny hidden beside your coffee table, and your subconscious mind will automatically recognize that you received more money. To the subconscious, your goal was achieved. Mission accomplished. No more work to be done! Even though consciously, you obviously meant more than one penny. Your subconscious mind will always take you literally. Therefore, you must be super specific with what you want.

So how do we set a proper goal?

Do you remember the acronym **S.M.A.R.T.** in the traditional goal setting sense? If you don't, basically each of the letters stands for a word to help guide you in creating a clearly written goal. S stands for specific; M stands for measurable; A stands for achievable; R stands for realistic; and T stands for time based. Unfortunately, this acronym bores me to tears, so I switched it up a little for us.

S= Specific, sexy, and simple

M= Measurable, motivating, and moving

A= Attainable (according to your belief system) and actionable

R= Realistic (according to your belief system), reassuring, and resonating

T= Time based, toward what you want, and transforming

When creating your 21-day goal, keep the fun version of **S.M.A.R.T.** in mind. Two things I wanted to mention about the words I chose for my own version of the acronym: Attainable and realistic are two words I normally dislike using. That's only because people take them way too literally and as a result set really small goal for themselves. So small that when they achieve them, they don't feel accomplished.

Absolutely nothing in your life is unrealistic or unattainable. If there is something that someone else has, it's physical proof that this exact same thing is possible for you too. We live in a level playing field world and no one is more special than you. No one is more worthy, more deserving, or more privileged than the next person. Please, remember that.

The reason why I left those words in this book anyway is because you will *not* achieve anything that you don't believe you can achieve. So, it is extremely important to keep in mind what you believe you are able to accomplish in a 21-day period. If it feels like too much of a stretch, it's not because it's impossible. It just means your belief muscle isn't strong enough yet to wrap your mind around it. And, that's okay! This is why this journal exists.

Remember I told you that we will be stretching your thinking? Our goal together is to start blowing your mind around what you truly are capable of.

I have a general goal setting formula that I like to use with my clients, and it has helped me tremendously in my own goal setting and achieving as well. I like to use this formula because it fits in with the **S.M.A.R.T.** acronym and it's very outcome focused. It's also something I picked up from my Neuro-Linguistic Programming Practitioner training.

The goal setting formula:

It is now ___(date)____ at __(time)___ and I am/have _____.

I see _____.

I hear _____.

I feel _____.

I have achieved this because _____.

In order to achieve this goal, these are the following tasks that I must make sure I accomplish by the decided time frame:

Task #1:	*Due Date:
Task #2:	Due Date:
Task #3:	Due Date:

*The above tasks and due dates must fall in the timeline of the main date chosen in the original goal setting formula

For the sake of this journal, you would choose your date to be 21 days from the moment you begin day one. Choose any area of your life, and choose something you'd really like to accomplish within that time frame. Make it meaningful to you and make it something that would actually make a big difference in your life when you finally accomplish it.

Some areas of your life may be:

Career/Finances
Health/Body
Family/Relationships
Spirituality
Fun/Recreation
Self-Growth/Personal Development
Lifestyle/Hobbies

To give you an example of a really great goal that someone can set for the next 21 days, it would look something like this:

Area of life to improve: Finances

What to improve specifically: Increase earnings by about $2,000 in my business

Why set this goal: It would allow me to go to Spain for a week the following month and be able to take my boyfriend with me

The goal written out using the formula: It is now September 17, 2017 at 11:11am and I have increased my income earnings by $2,356 in my business. I see the increase in sales coming through my PayPal account, and my email inbox filled with happy customers. I hear the excitement from my boyfriend yelling "woohoo" as I tell him that I just booked a 7-night trip to Spain for the two of us. I feel ecstatic, amazing, and full of life! I have achieved this because I decided to be resourceful, utilize Facebook ads, hire a marketing strategist, and create a new product to sell.

Tasks to achieve by September 17, 2017 and their due dates:

Task #1: I have written 36 emails reaching out to potential customers by August 25, 2017 about my current services.

Task #2: I have created a new service based around the ones that I currently have, but one that would appeal to a larger market priced at $250 per package by September 3rd, 2017.

Task #3: I have launched this new service by September 10th and have run two separate Facebook ads advertising the new service bringing in the 9 clients needed to reach my new financial goal.

Important Things to Note:

The 21-day goal as well as each of the 3 tasks are written in present tense. This is because goals that are written as if they have already happened are easier for the subconscious mind to accept as truth and to work on in order to help you manifest it.

Anything written in a format where it's evident it's not yet happened, will always and forever stay in the future. Again, this is because your subconscious mind takes everything literally. If you create a goal that says, "I will have ____," then you will *always* be in that place of "will have." Tomorrow will come and your goal is still going to sit in the future. You want your goal to sit in the present moment to involve your subconscious mind in the process.

Notice the specificity in the date, time, the goal itself, as well as the tasks. This is because the subconscious mind loves specifics. Instead of writing down 11:00am, we get specific with 11:11am. Instead of $2,000, we get specific with $2,356. Instead of 30 emails or 5 clients, we get more specific with 36 emails and 9 clients. Obviously, this is just an example, but my goal is to help you get clear on how to really involve your subconscious mind in your goal setting and goal achieving process.

Last thing to note is the "I have achieved this because ____" section at the end of the goal formula. This section is for your resources that are used in order to achieve this goal. What do you need to tap into in order to achieve it? Which resources will help you achieve it? Is it a mindset? A skill? A tool? A useful personality trait? Anything counts here, and if you don't know what resources you may need, ask someone who has achieved a similar goal as you. Noting your resources will help you get into action mode faster.

Set Your 21-Day Goal:

Now's the fun part! Using the formula shared with you, choose an outcome you would like to put into action over the next 21 days and use the guide below to help you format it into a physical goal.

Area of life to improve:

What to improve specifically:

Why set this goal:

The goal:

Write it in the space below using this formula:

It is now ___(date)_____ at __(time)___ and I am/have _____.

I see _____.

I hear _____.

I feel _____.

I have achieved this because _____.

In order to achieve this goal, these are the following tasks that I must make sure I accomplish by the decided time frame:

Task #1:	*Due Date:
Task #2:	Due Date:
Task #3:	Due Date

Yay! Now you're ready to start this 21-day journaling party.

Welcome to the ultimate 21-day journal for manifesting your kickass life.

I am so excited to watch your journey unfold and I hope you are too!

LET'S BEGIN!

Day 1 DATE: _____

Morning Section:

"IT'S NOT WHO YOU ARE THAT HOLDS YOU BACK. IT'S WHO YOU THINK YOU ARE NOT." – DENIS WAITLEY

What are you most grateful for today? List 5 things that first come to mind this morning:

What do you want to accomplish today? What's important for you to finish by the end of the day? What can you do today to get you one step closer to your goal?

If you could be, do, have anything you want in life, what would you want? Remember to DREAM BIG here. What desires would you like the Universe to work on today?

Do you believe that you are worthy of all of the incredible things that life has to offer you? If not, why not?

Set an intention for today:

What is your overall mood this morning? Why do you think that is?

Do you have anything to let go of before you start your day? Journal it out here to let out any frustrations, stresses, worries, or any other negative emotions that won't serve you today

Take a couple of minutes to meditate before you move on with your day. This can be as easy as taking 3-5 deep breaths in silence, or listen to the 5-minute guided meditation download provided. Once done, write down anything that came to mind. Share any inspirations that popped up from the space of stillness:

What is your biggest goal that you created from the goal setting workshop for the next 21 days? Write it down below to keep your subconscious mind focused on it throughout the day:

MORNING MANTRA OF THE *Day*

"No one is me, and **that** is my super power."

Repeat out loud 5 times with conviction to jumpstart your day with a piece of inspiring truth.

Evening Section:

Rate your day on a scale of 1-10, and explain why you chose the number that you did:

How can you make tomorrow even better?

One thing you can choose to improve upon to keep growing and becoming the best version of yourself:

Did you make any progress today toward your 21-day goal?

Did you accomplish everything you wanted to today? If not, how can you intend to do so tomorrow?

5 things you love and appreciate about yourself:

Let out anything about your day that isn't serving you before bed. This is a safe space to write about any frustrations, worries, doubts or fears so that you can go to bed in peace:

End your day with 3 wishes or desires. What would you like your subconscious mind to work on overnight? Are there any questions you would like answered by the Universe?

IF YOU WANT TO ACHIEVE GREATNESS STOP ASKING FOR

Permission

-ANONYMOUS

Day **2** DATE: _____

Morning Section:

"WHATEVER YOU ARE GRATEFUL FOR, YOU WILL SEE MORE OF IN YOUR LIFE. WHATEVER YOU TAKE FOR GRANTED, YOU WILL SEE LESS OF. IT'S LITERALLY UP TO YOU TO CHOOSE HOW MUCH GOOD YOU WANT TO SEE IN YOUR LIFE BASED ON THE AMOUNT OF GRATITUDE YOU HAVE FOR IT."- KATHRIN ZENKINA

What are you most grateful for today? List 5 things that first come to mind this morning:

What do you want to accomplish today? What's important for you to finish by the end of the day? What can you do today to get you one step closer to your goal?

What are your top desires that you would like the universe to work on today?

Is there someone or something you've been taking for granted that, if taken away, you would be extremely devastated and life would be completely different? Who is that person or what is that thing?

Set an intention for today:

What is your overall mood this morning? Why do you think that is?

Do you have anything to let go of before you start your day? Journal it out here to let out any frustrations, stresses, worries, or any other negative emotions that won't serve you today

Take a couple of minutes to meditate before you move on with your day. This can be as easy as taking 3-5 deep breaths in silence, or listen to the 5-minute guided meditation download provided. Once done, write down anything that came to mind. Share any inspirations that popped up from the space of stillness:

What is your biggest goal that you created from the goal setting workshop for the next 21 days? Write it down below to keep your subconscious mind focused on it throughout the day:

MORNING MANTRA OF THE *Day*

"Thank you, Universe, for all the blessings in my life. I choose to be grateful each and every single day."

Repeat out loud 5 times with conviction to jumpstart your day with a piece of inspiring truth.

Evening Section:

Rate your day on a scale of 1-10, and explain why you chose the number that you did:

How can you make tomorrow even better?

One thing you can choose to improve upon to keep growing and becoming the best version of yourself:

Did you make any progress today toward your 21-day goal?

Did you accomplish everything you wanted to today? If not, how can you intend to do so tomorrow?

5 things you love and appreciate about yourself:

Let out anything about your day that isn't serving you before bed. This is a safe space to write about any frustrations, worries, doubts or fears so that you can go to bed in peace:

End your day with 3 wishes or desires. What would you like your subconscious mind to work on overnight? Are there any questions you would like answered by the Universe?

I CAN'T THINK OF ANY BETTER

REPRESENTATION OF BEAUTY

THAN SOMEONE WHO IS

UNAFRAID TO BE

Herself.

- EMMA STONE

Day **3** DATE: _____

Morning Section:

"I AM- THE TWO MOST POWERFUL WORDS IN THE UNIVERSE. FOR WHAT FOLLOWS THEM, BECOMES YOUR DESTINY."
- UNKNOWN

What are you most grateful for today? List 5 things that first come to mind this morning:

What do you want to accomplish today? What's important for you to finish by the end of the day? What can you do today to get you one step closer to your goal?

What are your top desires that you would like the universe to work on today?

What do you usually say to yourself following the words "I am?" Most women find that the way they talk to themselves isn't so kind. In fact, when pointed out, they would find themselves horrified at the thought of saying the same things to their friends or someone that they love. Use the space below to explore your language patterns and see if they need to be changed:

Set an intention for today:

What is your overall mood this morning? Why do you think that is?

Do you have anything to let go of before you start your day? Journal it out here to let out any frustrations, stresses, worries, or any other negative emotions that won't serve you today

Take a couple of minutes to meditate before you move on with your day. This can be as easy as taking 3-5 deep breaths in silence, or listen to the 5-minute guided meditation download provided. Once done, write down anything that came to mind. Share any inspirations that popped up from the space of stillness:

What is your biggest goal that you created from the goal setting workshop for the next 21 days? Write it down below to keep your subconscious mind focused on it throughout the day:

MORNING MANTRA OF THE *Day*

"I am incredible, worthy, and deserving of everything I want and so much more."

Repeat out loud 5 times with conviction to jumpstart your day with a piece of inspiring truth.

Evening Section:

Rate your day on a scale of 1-10, and explain why you chose the number that you did:

How can you make tomorrow even better?

One thing you can choose to improve upon to keep growing and becoming the best version of yourself:

Did you make any progress today toward your 21-day goal?

Did you accomplish everything you wanted to today? If not, how can you intend to do so tomorrow?

5 things you love and appreciate about yourself:

Let out anything about your day that isn't serving you before bed. This is a safe space to write about any frustrations, worries, doubts or fears so that you can go to bed in peace:

End your day with 3 wishes or desires. What would you like your subconscious mind to work on overnight? Are there any questions you would like answered by the Universe?

FORGET ABOUT THE FAST
LANE. IF YOU REALLY WANT
TO FLY, JUST HARNESS YOUR
POWER TO YOUR

Passion

-OPRAH WINFREY

SHE'S **KILLIN'** IT

Day **4** DATE: _____

Morning Section:

**"IF IT'S STILL IN YOUR MIND, IT'S WORTH TAKING THE RISK."
- PAULO COELHO**

What are you most grateful for today? List 5 things that first come to mind this morning:

What do you want to accomplish today? What's important for you to finish by the end of the day? What can you do today to get you one step closer to your goal?

What are your top desires that you would like the universe to work on today?

You are 85 years old sitting on a rocking chair looking back at your life. All of the years from now until then you have already lived. What kind of memories are you glad that you have made? What accomplishments are you most proud of? What kind of risks are you glad that you took?

Set an intention for today:

What is your overall mood this morning? Why do you think that is?

Do you have anything to let go of before you start your day? Journal it out here to let out any frustrations, stresses, worries, or any other negative emotions that won't serve you today

Take a couple of minutes to meditate before you move on with your day. This can be as easy as taking 3-5 deep breaths in silence, or listen to the 5-minute guided meditation download provided. Once done, write down anything that came to mind. Share any inspirations that popped up from the space of stillness:

What is your biggest goal that you created from the goal setting workshop for the next 21 days? Write it down below to keep your subconscious mind focused on it throughout the day:

MORNING MANTRA OF THE *Day*

"I am always divinely guided, loved, and protected."

Repeat out loud 5 times with conviction to jumpstart your day with a piece of inspiring truth.

Evening Section:

Rate your day on a scale of 1-10, and explain why you chose the number that you did:

How can you make tomorrow even better?

One thing you can choose to improve upon to keep growing and becoming the best version of yourself:

Did you make any progress today toward your 21-day goal?

Did you accomplish everything you wanted to today? If not, how can you intend to do so tomorrow?

5 things you love and appreciate about yourself

Let out anything about your day that isn't serving you before bed. This is a safe space to write about any frustrations, worries, doubts or fears so that you can go to bed in peace:

End your day with 3 wishes or desires. What would you like your subconscious mind to work on overnight? Are there any questions you would like answered by the Universe?

OPTIMISM IS THE FAITH THAT LEADS TO *Achievement*

-HELEN KELLER

Day **5** DATE: _____

Morning Section:

"SETTING GOALS WITH NO INTENTION WILL LEAD YOU SPIN YOUR WHEELS. SETTING INTENTIONS WITH NO GOALS WILL LEAVE YOU LOST IN FANTASY LAND. BEING INTENTIONAL WITH YOUR GOALS, HOWEVER, WILL CREATE THE MAGICAL LIFE YOU'VE ALWAYS DREAMED OF. –KATHRIN ZENKINA

What are you most grateful for today? List 5 things that first come to mind this morning:

What do you want to accomplish today? What's important for you to finish by the end of the day? What can you do today to get you one step closer to your goal?

What are your top desires that you would like the universe to work on today?

Is there currently something in your life that you've sat on for years, hesitating? What is it? And how can you get intentional with it, set a goal, and finally take action?

Set an intention for today:

What is your overall mood this morning? Why do you think that is?

Do you have anything to let go of before you start your day? Journal it out here to let out any frustrations, stresses, worries, or any other negative emotions that won't serve you today

Take a couple of minutes to meditate before you move on with your day. This can be as easy as taking 3-5 deep breaths in silence, or listen to the 5-minute guided meditation download provided. Once done, write down anything that came to mind. Share any inspirations that popped up from the space of stillness:

What is your biggest goal that you created from the goal setting workshop for the next 21 days? Write it down below to keep your subconscious mind focused on it throughout the day:

MORNING MANTRA OF THE *Day*

"I achieve everything I want in my life with ease."

Repeat out loud 5 times with conviction to jumpstart your day with a piece of inspiring truth.

Evening Section:

Rate your day on a scale of 1-10, and explain why you chose the number that you did:

How can you make tomorrow even better?

One thing you can choose to improve upon to keep growing and becoming the best version of yourself:

Did you make any progress today toward your 21-day goal?

Did you accomplish everything you wanted to today? If not, how can you intend to do so tomorrow?

5 things you love and appreciate about yourself:

Let out anything about your day that isn't serving you before bed. This is a safe space to write about any frustrations, worries, doubts or fears so that you can go to bed in peace:

End your day with 3 wishes or desires. What would you like your subconscious mind to work on overnight? Are there any questions you would like answered by the Universe?

YOU ARE THE ONE THAT POSSESSES
THE KEYS TO YOUR BEING. YOU
CARRY THE PASSPORT TO YOUR
OWN

Happiness

- DIANE VON FURSTENBERG

Day **6** DATE: _____

Morning Section:

"SUCCESS DOESN'T COME FROM WHAT YOU DO OCCASIONALLY. IT COMES FROM WHAT YOU DO CONSISTENTLY." –MARIE FORLEO

What are you most grateful for today? List 5 things that first come to mind this morning:

What do you want to accomplish today? What's important for you to finish by the end of the day? What can you do today to get you one step closer to your goal?

What are your top desires that you would like the universe to work on today?

Part of progressing in life is growing into the best version of yourself so that you can contribute more to others and the world around you in the greatest way possible. Who is the best version of you? What is that version of yourself like? And how can you work every single day to become her?

Set an intention for today:

What is your overall mood this morning? Why do you think that is?

Do you have anything to let go of before you start your day? Journal it out here to let out any frustrations, stresses, worries, or any other negative emotions that won't serve you today

Take a couple of minutes to meditate before you move on with your day. This can be as easy as taking 3-5 deep breaths in silence, or listen to the 5-minute guided meditation download provided. Once done, write down anything that came to mind. Share any inspirations that popped up from the space of stillness:

What is your biggest goal that you created from the goal setting workshop for the next 21 days? Write it down below to keep your subconscious mind focused on it throughout the day:

MORNING MANTRA OF THE *Day*

"Becoming the best version of myself is so easy, so natural, and it feels so good to me."

Repeat out loud 5 times with conviction to jumpstart your day with a piece of inspiring truth.

Evening Section:

Rate your day on a scale of 1-10, and explain why you chose the number that you did:

How can you make tomorrow even better?

One thing you can choose to improve upon to keep growing and becoming the best version of yourself:

Did you make any progress today toward your 21-day goal?

Did you accomplish everything you wanted to today? If not, how can you intend to do so tomorrow?

5 things you love and appreciate about yourself:

Let out anything about your day that isn't serving you before bed. This is a safe space to write about any frustrations, worries, doubts or fears so that you can go to bed in peace:

End your day with 3 wishes or desires. What would you like your subconscious mind to work on overnight? Are there any questions you would like answered by the Universe?

IF YOU DON'T LIKE THE ROAD
YOU'RE WALKING, START PAVING
ANOTHER *one*

- DOLLY PARTON

Day **7** DATE: _____

Morning Section:

"THE KEY TO ABUNDANCE IS MEETING LIMITED CIRCUMSTANCES WITH UNLIMITED THOUGHTS." –MARIANNE WILLIAMSON

What are you most grateful for today? List 5 things that first come to mind this morning:

What do you want to accomplish today? What's important for you to finish by the end of the day? What can you do today to get you one step closer to your goal?

What are your top desires that you would like the universe to work on today?

Fill in the blanks: Money is _____; Money allows me to _____; Money supports me by _____. Is your viewpoint on money more of a positive one or negative one? Why do you think that is?

Set an intention for today:

What is your overall mood this morning? Why do you think that is?

Do you have anything to let go of before you start your day? Journal it out here to let out any frustrations, stresses, worries, or any other negative emotions that won't serve you today

Take a couple of minutes to meditate before you move on with your day. This can be as easy as taking 3-5 deep breaths in silence, or listen to the 5-minute guided meditation download provided. Once done, write down anything that came to mind. Share any inspirations that popped up from the space of stillness:

What is your biggest goal that you created from the goal setting workshop for the next 21 days? Write it down below to keep your subconscious mind focused on it throughout the day:

MORNING MANTRA OF THE *Day*

"I choose to believe that money is an unlimited resource and it is always flowing my way."

Repeat out loud 5 times with conviction to jumpstart your day with a piece of inspiring truth.

Evening Section:

Rate your day on a scale of 1-10, and explain why you chose the number that you did:

How can you make tomorrow even better?

One thing you can choose to improve upon to keep growing and becoming the best version of yourself:

Did you make any progress today toward your 21-day goal?

Did you accomplish everything you wanted to today? If not, how can you intend to do so tomorrow?

5 things you love and appreciate about yourself:

Let out anything about your day that isn't serving you before bed. This is a safe space to write about any frustrations, worries, doubts or fears so that you can go to bed in peace:

End your day with 3 wishes or desires. What would you like your subconscious mind to work on overnight? Are there any questions you would like answered by the Universe?

THE PESSIMIST SEES DIFFICULTY IN EVERY
OPPORTUNITY. THE OPTIMIST SEES THE
OPPORTUNITY IN EVERY *difficulty*

- WINSTON CHURCHILL

Day **8** DATE: _____

Morning Section:

"REMEMBER YOUR DREAMS AND FIGHT FOR THEM. YOU MUST KNOW WHAT YOU WANT FROM LIFE. THERE IS JUST ONE THING THAT MAKES YOUR DREAM BECOME IMPOSSIBLE: THE FEAR OF FAILURE." -PAULO COELHO

What are you most grateful for today? List 5 things that first come to mind this morning:

What do you want to accomplish today? What's important for you to finish by the end of the day? What can you do today to get you one step closer to your goal?

What are your top desires that you would like the universe to work on today?

If money was no object, and you could go to 5 different locations anywhere in the world, where would you go and why?

Set an intention for today:

What is your overall mood this morning? Why do you think that is?

Do you have anything to let go of before you start your day? Journal it out here to let out any frustrations, stresses, worries, or any other negative emotions that won't serve you today

Take a couple of minutes to meditate before you move on with your day. This can be as easy as taking 3-5 deep breaths in silence, or listen to the 5-minute guided meditation download provided. Once done, write down anything that came to mind. Share any inspirations that popped up from the space of stillness:

What is your biggest goal that you created from the goal setting workshop for the next 21 days? Write it down below to keep your subconscious mind focused on it throughout the day:

MORNING MANTRA OF THE *Day*

"The sky's the limit and the world is my oyster. I can be, do, have anything I want in my life."

Repeat out loud 5 times with conviction to jumpstart your day with a piece of inspiring truth.

Evening Section:

Rate your day on a scale of 1-10, and explain why you chose the number that you did:

How can you make tomorrow even better?

One thing you can choose to improve upon to keep growing and becoming the best version of yourself:

Did you make any progress today toward your 21-day goal?

Did you accomplish everything you wanted to today? If not, how can you intend to do so tomorrow?

5 things you love and appreciate about yourself:

Let out anything about your day that isn't serving you before bed. This is a safe space to write about any frustrations, worries, doubts or fears so that you can go to bed in peace:

End your day with 3 wishes or desires. What would you like your subconscious mind to work on overnight? Are there any questions you would like answered by the Universe?

I'D RATHER REGRET THE THINGS I'VE DONE THAN
REGRET THE THINGS I HAVEN'T

done

- LUCILLE BALL

Day **9** DATE: _____

Morning Section:

"NO ONE CAN MAKE YOU FEEL INFERIOR WITHOUT YOUR CONSENT." –ELEANOR ROOSEVELT

What are you most grateful for today? List 5 things that first come to mind this morning:

What do you want to accomplish today? What's important for you to finish by the end of the day? What can you do today to get you one step closer to your goal?

What are your top desires that you would like the universe to work on today?

Is there anyone in your life making you feel inferior? Why is that? And better yet, why are you letting them?

Set an intention for today:

What is your overall mood this morning? Why do you think that is?

Do you have anything to let go of before you start your day? Journal it out here to let out any frustrations, stresses, worries, or any other negative emotions that won't serve you today

Take a couple of minutes to meditate before you move on with your day. This can be as easy as taking 3-5 deep breaths in silence, or listen to the 5-minute guided meditation download provided. Once done, write down anything that came to mind. Share any inspirations that popped up from the space of stillness:

What is your biggest goal that you created from the goal setting workshop for the next 21 days? Write it down below to keep your subconscious mind focused on it throughout the day:

MORNING MANTRA OF THE *Day*

"I give myself permission to shine brighter than the sun."

Repeat out loud 5 times with conviction to jumpstart your day with a piece of inspiring truth.

Evening Section:

Rate your day on a scale of 1-10, and explain why you chose the number that you did:

How can you make tomorrow even better?

One thing you can choose to improve upon to keep growing and becoming the best version of yourself:

Did you make any progress today toward your 21-day goal?

Did you accomplish everything you wanted to today? If not, how can you intend to do so tomorrow?

5 things you love and appreciate about yourself:

Let out anything about your day that isn't serving you before bed. This is a safe space to write about any frustrations, worries, doubts or fears so that you can go to bed in peace:

End your day with 3 wishes or desires. What would you like your subconscious mind to work on overnight? Are there any questions you would like answered by the Universe?

STEP OUT OF THE HISTORY THAT IS
HOLDING YOU BACK. STEP INTO THE
NEW STORY YOU ARE WILLING TO *create*

- OPRAH WINFREY

Day **10** DATE: _____

Morning Section:

"SUCCESS SEEMS TO BE LARGELY A MATTER OF HANGING ON AFTER OTHERS HAVE LET GO." –WILLIAM FEATHER

What are you most grateful for today? List 5 things that first come to mind this morning:

What do you want to accomplish today? What's important for you to finish by the end of the day? What can you do today to get you one step closer to your goal?

What are your top desires that you would like the universe to work on today?

What does success look like to you? Create your definition of success.

Set an intention for today:

What is your overall mood this morning? Why do you think that is?

Do you have anything to let go of before you start your day? Journal it out here to let out any frustrations, stresses, worries, or any other negative emotions that won't serve you today

Take a couple of minutes to meditate before you move on with your day. This can be as easy as taking 3-5 deep breaths in silence, or listen to the 5-minute guided meditation download provided. Once done, write down anything that came to mind. Share any inspirations that popped up from the space of stillness:

What is your biggest goal that you created from the goal setting workshop for the next 21 days? Write it down below to keep your subconscious mind focused on it throughout the day:

MORNING MANTRA OF THE *Day*

"I am already wildly successful and my version of success feels SO good to me."

Repeat out loud 5 times with conviction to jumpstart your day with a piece of inspiring truth.

Evening Section:

Rate your day on a scale of 1-10, and explain why you chose the number that you did:

How can you make tomorrow even better?

One thing you can choose to improve upon to keep growing and becoming the best version of yourself:

Did you make any progress today toward your 21-day goal?

Did you accomplish everything you wanted to today? If not, how can you intend to do so tomorrow?

5 things you love and appreciate about yourself:

Let out anything about your day that isn't serving you before bed. This is a safe space to write about any frustrations, worries, doubts or fears so that you can go to bed in peace:

End your day with 3 wishes or desires. What would you like your subconscious mind to work on overnight? Are there any questions you would like answered by the Universe?

A REAL DECISION IS MEASURED BY THE FACT THAT YOU'VE TAKEN A NEW ACTION. IF THERE'S NO ACTION, YOU HAVEN'T TRULY *decided*

– TONY ROBBINS

Day **11** DATE: _____

Morning Section:

"THE BEST AND MOST BEAUTIFUL THINGS IN THE WORLD CANNOT BE SEEN OR EVEN TOUCHED-THEY MUST BE FELT WITH THE HEART." –HELEN KELLER

What are you most grateful for today? List 5 things that first come to mind this morning:

What do you want to accomplish today? What's important for you to finish by the end of the day? What can you do today to get you one step closer to your goal?

What are your top desires that you would like the universe to work on today?

What is one of your most significant and cherished memories in your life? Why is it so significant?

Set an intention for today:

What is your overall mood this morning? Why do you think that is?

Do you have anything to let go of before you start your day? Journal it out here to let out any frustrations, stresses, worries, or any other negative emotions that won't serve you today

Take a couple of minutes to meditate before you move on with your day. This can be as easy as taking 3-5 deep breaths in silence, or listen to the 5-minute guided meditation download provided. Once done, write down anything that came to mind. Share any inspirations that popped up from the space of stillness:

What is your biggest goal that you created from the goal setting workshop for the next 21 days? Write it down below to keep your subconscious mind focused on it throughout the day:

MORNING MANTRA OF THE *Day*

"The desires of the heart are meant to manifest. I can rejoice in knowing that all my desires are on their way to me."

Repeat out loud 5 times with conviction to jumpstart your day with a piece of inspiring truth.

Evening Section:

Rate your day on a scale of 1-10, and explain why you chose the number that you did:

How can you make tomorrow even better?

One thing you can choose to improve upon to keep growing and becoming the best version of yourself:

Did you make any progress today toward your 21-day goal?

Did you accomplish everything you wanted to today? If not, how can you intend to do so tomorrow?

5 things you love and appreciate about yourself:

Let out anything about your day that isn't serving you before bed. This is a safe space to write about any frustrations, worries, doubts or fears so that you can go to bed in peace:

End your day with 3 wishes or desires. What would you like your subconscious mind to work on overnight? Are there any questions you would like answered by the Universe?

PEOPLE ARE NOT LAZY. THEY SIMPLY
HAVE IMPOTENT GOALS - THAT IS, GOALS
THAT DO NOT INSPIRE *them*

– TONY ROBBINS

Day **12** DATE: _____

Morning Section:

"THE WEAK CAN NEVER FORGIVE. FORGIVENESS IS THE ATTRIBUTE OF THE STRONG." –MAHATMA GANDHI

What are you most grateful for today? List 5 things that first come to mind this morning:

What do you want to accomplish today? What's important for you to finish by the end of the day? What can you do today to get you one step closer to your goal?

What are your top desires that you would like the universe to work on today?

What do I need to forgive myself for? What do I need to forgive others for?

Set an intention for today:

What is your overall mood this morning? Why do you think that is?

Do you have anything to let go of before you start your day? Journal it out here to let out any frustrations, stresses, worries, or any other negative emotions that won't serve you today:

Take a couple of minutes to meditate before you move on with your day. This can be as easy as taking 3-5 deep breaths in silence, or listen to the 5-minute guided meditation download provided. Once done, write down anything that came to mind. Share any inspirations that popped up from the space of stillness:

What is your biggest goal that you created from the goal setting workshop for the next 21 days? Write it down below to keep your subconscious mind focused on it throughout the day:

MORNING MANTRA OF THE Day

"The more I forgive, the freer I feel."

Repeat out loud 5 times with conviction to jumpstart your day with a piece of inspiring truth.

Evening Section:

Rate your day on a scale of 1-10, and explain why you chose the number that you did:

How can you make tomorrow even better?

One thing you can choose to improve upon to keep growing and becoming the best version of yourself:

Did you make any progress today toward your 21-day goal?

Did you accomplish everything you wanted to today? If not, how can you intend to do so tomorrow?

5 things you love and appreciate about yourself:

Let out anything about your day that isn't serving you before bed. This is a safe space to write about any frustrations, worries, doubts or fears so that you can go to bed in peace:

End your day with 3 wishes or desires. What would you like your subconscious mind to work on overnight? Are there any questions you would like answered by the Universe?

THE MOST EFFECTIVE WAY TO
DO IT, IS TO DO *it*

–AMELIA EARHART

Day **13** DATE: _____

Morning Section:

"PLEASE THINK ABOUT YOUR LEGACY, BECAUSE YOU'RE WRITING IT EVERY DAY." –GARY VAYNERCHUCK

What are you most grateful for today? List 5 things that first come to mind this morning:

What do you want to accomplish today? What's important for you to finish by the end of the day? What can you do today to get you one step closer to your goal?

What are your top desires that you would like the universe to work on today?

What do you want your legacy to be? What would make you incredibly happy to know that you are leaving others with on your very last day on Earth?

Set an intention for today:

What is your overall mood this morning? Why do you think that is?

Do you have anything to let go of before you start your day? Journal it out here to let out any frustrations, stresses, worries, or any other negative emotions that won't serve you today

Take a couple of minutes to meditate before you move on with your day. This can be as easy as taking 3-5 deep breaths in silence, or listen to the 5-minute guided meditation download provided. Once done, write down anything that came to mind. Share any inspirations that popped up from the space of stillness:

What is your biggest goal that you created from the goal setting workshop for the next 21 days? Write it down below to keep your subconscious mind focused on it throughout the day:

MORNING MANTRA OF THE *Day*

"I am enough, have always been enough, and will always be enough."

Repeat out loud 5 times with conviction to jumpstart your day with a piece of inspiring truth.

Evening Section:

Rate your day on a scale of 1-10, and explain why you chose the number that you did:

How can you make tomorrow even better?

One thing you can choose to improve upon to keep growing and becoming the best version of yourself:

Did you make any progress today toward your 21-day goal?

Did you accomplish everything you wanted to today? If not, how can you intend to do so tomorrow?

SHE'S **KILLIN'** IT

5 things you love and appreciate about yourself:

Let out anything about your day that isn't serving you before bed. This is a safe space to write about any frustrations, worries, doubts or fears so that you can go to bed in peace:

End your day with 3 wishes or desires. What would you like your subconscious mind to work on overnight? Are there any questions you would like answered by the Universe?

THE POWER YOU HAVE IS TO BE THE BEST
VERSION OF YOURSELF YOU CAN BE, SO YOU
CAN CREATE A BETTER *world*

–ASHLEY RICKARDS

Day **14** DATE: _____

Morning Section:

**IF YOU WANT LOVE AND ABUNDANCE IN YOUR LIFE, GIVE IT AWAY.
—MARK TWAIN**

What are you most grateful for today? List 5 things that first come to mind this morning:

What do you want to accomplish today? What's important for you to finish by the end of the day? What can you do today to get you one step closer to your goal?

What are your top desires that you would like the universe to work on today?

What can you do today to add value to others, yourself, and the world around you?

Set an intention for today:

What is your overall mood this morning? Why do you think that is?

Do you have anything to let go of before you start your day? Journal it out here to let out any frustrations, stresses, worries, or any other negative emotions that won't serve you today:

Take a couple of minutes to meditate before you move on with your day. This can be as easy as taking 3-5 deep breaths in silence, or listen to the 5-minute guided meditation download provided. Once done, write down anything that came to mind. Share any inspirations that popped up from the space of stillness:

What is your biggest goal that you created from the goal setting workshop for the next 21 days? Write it down below to keep your subconscious mind focused on it throughout the day:

MORNING MANTRA OF THE *Day*

"The more value I give, the more abundance I will receive.

Repeat out loud 5 times with conviction to jumpstart your day with a piece of inspiring truth.

Evening Section:

Rate your day on a scale of 1-10, and explain why you chose the number that you did:

How can you make tomorrow even better?

One thing you can choose to improve upon to keep growing and becoming the best version of yourself:

Did you make any progress today toward your 21-day goal?

Did you accomplish everything you wanted to today? If not, how can you intend to do so tomorrow?

5 things you love and appreciate about yourself:

Let out anything about your day that isn't serving you before bed. This is a safe space to write about any frustrations, worries, doubts or fears so that you can go to bed in peace:

End your day with 3 wishes or desires. What would you like your subconscious mind to work on overnight? Are there any questions you would like answered by the Universe?

IF YOU ARE WORKING ON SOMETHING THAT
YOU REALLY CARE ABOUT, YOU DON'T HAVE TO
BE PUSHED. THE VISION PULLS *you*

−STEVE JOBS

Day **15** DATE: _____

Morning Section:

"SHE WAS UNSTOPPABLE NOT BECAUSE SHE DID NOT HAVE FAILURES OR DOUBTS, BUT BECAUSE SHE CONTINUED ON DESPITE THEM." –BEAU TAPLIN

What are you most grateful for today? List 5 things that first come to mind this morning:

What do you want to accomplish today? What's important for you to finish by the end of the day? What can you do today to get you one step closer to your goal?

What are your top desires that you would like the universe to work on today?

Write a love letter to yourself. Infuse this letter with as much loving energy as you could possibly ooze into the space below. You deserve it!

Set an intention for today:

What is your overall mood this morning? Why do you think that is?

Do you have anything to let go of before you start your day? Journal it out here to let out any frustrations, stresses, worries, or any other negative emotions that won't serve you today:

Take a couple of minutes to meditate before you move on with your day. This can be as easy as taking 3-5 deep breaths in silence, or listen to the 5-minute guided meditation download provided. Once done, write down anything that came to mind. Share any inspirations that popped up from the space of stillness:

What is your biggest goal that you created from the goal setting workshop for the next 21 days? Write it down below to keep your subconscious mind focused on it throughout the day:

MORNING MANTRA OF THE *Day*

"I choose to forgive myself and shower myself with endless love.'

Repeat out loud 5 times with conviction to jumpstart your day with a piece of inspiring truth.

Evening Section:

Rate your day on a scale of 1-10, and explain why you chose the number that you did:

How can you make tomorrow even better?

One thing you can choose to improve upon to keep growing and becoming the best version of yourself:

Did you make any progress today toward your 21-day goal?

Did you accomplish everything you wanted to today? If not, how can you intend to do so tomorrow?

5 things you love and appreciate about yourself:

Let out anything about your day that isn't serving you before bed. This is a safe space to write about any frustrations, worries, doubts or fears so that you can go to bed in peace:

End your day with 3 wishes or desires. What would you like your subconscious mind to work on overnight? Are there any questions you would like answered by the Universe?

ALL OUR DREAMS CAN COME TRUE IF WE HAVE
THE COURAGE TO PURSUE *them*

-WALT DISNEY

Day **16** DATE: _____

Morning Section:

"NEVER LET THE SADNESS OF YOUR PAST AND THE FEAR OF YOUR FUTURE RUIN THE HAPPINESS OF YOUR PRESENT." –UNKNOWN

What are you most grateful for today? List 5 things that first come to mind this morning:

What do you want to accomplish today? What's important for you to finish by the end of the day? What can you do today to get you one step closer to your goal?

What are your top desires that you would like the universe to work on today?

What is your biggest fear in life? Is it possible to overcome this fear, and if it is, how would you do it?

Set an intention for today:

What is your overall mood this morning? Why do you think that is?

Do you have anything to let go of before you start your day? Journal it out here to let out any frustrations, stresses, worries, or any other negative emotions that won't serve you today:

Take a couple of minutes to meditate before you move on with your day. This can be as easy as taking 3-5 deep breaths in silence, or listen to the 5-minute guided meditation download provided. Once done, write down anything that came to mind. Share any inspirations that popped up from the space of stillness:

What is your biggest goal that you created from the goal setting workshop for the next 21 days? Write it down below to keep your subconscious mind focused on it throughout the day:

MORNING MANTRA OF THE *Day*

"I choose to be fearless in all pursuits that light my soul up on fire."

Repeat out loud 5 times with conviction to jumpstart your day with a piece of inspiring truth.

Evening Section:

Rate your day on a scale of 1-10, and explain why you chose the number that you did:

How can you make tomorrow even better?

One thing you can choose to improve upon to keep growing and becoming the best version of yourself:

Did you make any progress today toward your 21-day goal?

Did you accomplish everything you wanted to today? If not, how can you intend to do so tomorrow?

5 things you love and appreciate about yourself:

Let out anything about your day that isn't serving you before bed. This is a safe space to write about any frustrations, worries, doubts or fears so that you can go to bed in peace:

End your day with 3 wishes or desires. What would you like your subconscious mind to work on overnight? Are there any questions you would like answered by the Universe?

EVERYTHING YOU CAN IMAGINE IS *real*

-PABLO PICASSO

Day **17** DATE: _____

Morning Section:

"MY MISSION IN LIFE IS NOT MERELY TO SURVIVE, BUT TO THRIVE; AND TO DO SO WITH SOME PASSION, SOME COMPASSION, SOME HUMOR, AND SOME STYLE." –MAYA ANGELOU

What are you most grateful for today? List 5 things that first come to mind this morning:

What do you want to accomplish today? What's important for you to finish by the end of the day? What can you do today to get you one step closer to your goal?

What are your top desires that you would like the universe to work on today?

Do you have a mission statement for yourself? If not, create one today. How do you want to live your life on a consistent basis?

Set an intention for today:

What is your overall mood this morning? Why do you think that is?

Do you have anything to let go of before you start your day? Journal it out here to let out any frustrations, stresses, worries, or any other negative emotions that won't serve you today

Take a couple of minutes to meditate before you move on with your day. This can be as easy as taking 3-5 deep breaths in silence, or listen to the 5-minute guided meditation download provided. Once done, write down anything that came to mind. Share any inspirations that popped up from the space of stillness:

What is your biggest goal that you created from the goal setting workshop for the next 21 days? Write it down below to keep your subconscious mind focused on it throughout the day:

MORNING MANTRA OF THE *Day*

"My life is nothing but one big blessing after another."

Repeat out loud 5 times with conviction to jumpstart your day with a piece of inspiring truth.

Evening Section:

Rate your day on a scale of 1-10, and explain why you chose the number that you did:

How can you make tomorrow even better?

One thing you can choose to improve upon to keep growing and becoming the best version of yourself:

Did you make any progress today toward your 21-day goal?

Did you accomplish everything you wanted to today? If not, how can you intend to do so tomorrow?

5 things you love and appreciate about yourself:

Let out anything about your day that isn't serving you before bed. This is a safe space to write about any frustrations, worries, doubts or fears so that you can go to bed in peace:

End your day with 3 wishes or desires. What would you like your subconscious mind to work on overnight? Are there any questions you would like answered by the Universe?

SETTING GOALS IS THE FIRST STEP IN TURNING THE INVISIBLE INTO THE *visible*

–TONY ROBBINS

Day **18** DATE: _____

Morning Section:

"IF YOU WERE ABLE TO BELIEVE IN SANTA CLAUS FOR 8 YEARS, YOU CAN BELIEVE IN YOURSELF FOR 5 MINUTES." -UNKNOWN

What are you most grateful for today? List 5 things that first come to mind this morning:

What do you want to accomplish today? What's important for you to finish by the end of the day? What can you do today to get you one step closer to your goal?

What are your top desires that you would like the universe to work on today?

What is the greatest cause of stress, overwhelm, and worry in your life? What can you do to start eliminating the sources of these feelings in your everyday life? Or, at least, changing the way that you feel about the sources? Can you reframe them in any way?

Set an intention for today:

What is your overall mood this morning? Why do you think that is?

Do you have anything to let go of before you start your day? Journal it out here to let out any frustrations, stresses, worries, or any other negative emotions that won't serve you today

Take a couple of minutes to meditate before you move on with your day. This can be as easy as taking 3-5 deep breaths in silence, or listen to the 5-minute guided meditation download provided. Once done, write down anything that came to mind. Share any inspirations that popped up from the space of stillness:

What is your biggest goal that you created from the goal setting workshop for the next 21 days? Write it down below to keep your subconscious mind focused on it throughout the day:

MORNING MANTRA OF THE *Day*

"I choose to release all negative emotions that no longer serve me. It's my time to start feeling good."

Repeat out loud 5 times with conviction to jumpstart your day with a piece of inspiring truth.

Evening Section:

Rate your day on a scale of 1-10, and explain why you chose the number that you did:

How can you make tomorrow even better?

One thing you can choose to improve upon to keep growing and becoming the best version of yourself:

Did you make any progress today toward your 21-day goal?

Did you accomplish everything you wanted to today? If not, how can you intend to do so tomorrow?

5 things you love and appreciate about yourself:

Let out anything about your day that isn't serving you before bed. This is a safe space to write about any frustrations, worries, doubts or fears so that you can go to bed in peace:

End your day with 3 wishes or desires. What would you like your subconscious mind to work on overnight? Are there any questions you would like answered by the Universe?

THERE ARE NO UNREALISTIC DREAMS,
JUST UNREALISTIC

timelines

-NIDO QUBEIN

Day **19** DATE: _____

Morning Section:

"BUT THE REAL SECRET TO LIFELONG GOOD HEALTH IS ACTUALLY THE OPPOSITE: LET YOUR BODY TAKE CARE OF YOU." – DEEPAK CHOPRA

What are you most grateful for today? List 5 things that first come to mind this morning:

What do you want to accomplish today? What's important for you to finish by the end of the day? What can you do today to get you one step closer to your goal?

What are your top desires that you would like the universe to work on today?

Do you believe you are the healthiest version of yourself you could possibly be?
If not, what needs to change? If so, how can you go one step further into your
health & wellness journey?

Set an intention for today:

What is your overall mood this morning? Why do you think that is?

Do you have anything to let go of before you start your day? Journal it out here to let out any frustrations, stresses, worries, or any other negative emotions that won't serve you today:

Take a couple of minutes to meditate before you move on with your day. This can be as easy as taking 3-5 deep breaths in silence, or listen to the 5-minute guided meditation download provided. Once done, write down anything that came to mind. Share any inspirations that popped up from the space of stillness:

What is your biggest goal that you created from the goal setting workshop for the next 21 days? Write it down below to keep your subconscious mind focused on it throughout the day:

MORNING MANTRA OF THE *Day*

"My health is my wealth. I love my body, and my body loves me."

Repeat out loud 5 times with conviction to jumpstart your day with a piece of inspiring truth.

Evening Section:

Rate your day on a scale of 1-10, and explain why you chose the number that you did:

How can you make tomorrow even better?

One thing you can choose to improve upon to keep growing and becoming the best version of yourself:

Did you make any progress today toward your 21-day goal?

Did you accomplish everything you wanted to today? If not, how can you intend to do so tomorrow?

5 things you love and appreciate about yourself:

Let out anything about your day that isn't serving you before bed. This is a safe space to write about any frustrations, worries, doubts or fears so that you can go to bed in peace:

End your day with 3 wishes or desires. What would you like your subconscious mind to work on overnight? Are there any questions you would like answered by the Universe?

IF YOU CHANGE THE WAY YOU LOOK AT THINGS,
THE THINGS YOU LOOK AT

change

-DR. WAYNE DYER

Day **20** DATE: _____

Morning Section:

"I WANT TO CHALLENGE YOU TODAY TO GET OUT OF YOUR COMFORT ZONE. YOU HAVE SO MUCH INCREDIBLE POTENTIAL ON THE INSIDE. GOD HAS PUT GIFTS AND TALENTS IN YOU THAT YOU PROBABLY DON'T KNOW ANYTHING ABOUT." –JOEL OSTEEN

What are you most grateful for today? List 5 things that first come to mind this morning:

What do you want to accomplish today? What's important for you to finish by the end of the day? What can you do today to get you one step closer to your goal?

What are your top desires that you would like the universe to work on today?

How often do you take yourself out of your comfort zone? What is one thing you can do today to take yourself out of your comfort zone and, as a result, expand it?

Set an intention for today:

What is your overall mood this morning? Why do you think that is?

Do you have anything to let go of before you start your day? Journal it out here to let out any frustrations, stresses, worries, or any other negative emotions that won't serve you today

Take a couple of minutes to meditate before you move on with your day. This can be as easy as taking 3-5 deep breaths in silence, or listen to the 5-minute guided meditation download provided. Once done, write down anything that came to mind. Share any inspirations that popped up from the space of stillness:

What is your biggest goal that you created from the goal setting workshop for the next 21 days? Write it down below to keep your subconscious mind focused on it throughout the day:

MORNING MANTRA OF THE *Day*

"It is completely safe for me to grow and expand past my comfort zone."

Repeat out loud 5 times with conviction to jumpstart your day with a piece of inspiring truth.

Evening Section:

Rate your day on a scale of 1-10, and explain why you chose the number that you did:

How can you make tomorrow even better?

One thing you can choose to improve upon to keep growing and becoming the best version of yourself:

Did you make any progress today toward your 21-day goal?

Did you accomplish everything you wanted to today? If not, how can you intend to do so tomorrow?

5 things you love and appreciate about yourself:

Let out anything about your day that isn't serving you before bed. This is a safe space to write about any frustrations, worries, doubts or fears so that you can go to bed in peace:

End your day with 3 wishes or desires. What would you like your subconscious mind to work on overnight? Are there any questions you would like answered by the Universe?

IT'S ONE OF THE GREATEST GIFTS YOU CAN GIVE YOURSELF, TO FORGIVE. FORGIVE *everybody*

- MAYA ANGELOU

Day **21** DATE: _____

Morning Section:

"WHEN YOU WANT SOMETHING, ALL THE UNIVERSE CONSPIRES IN HELPING YOU TO ACHIEVE IT." – PAULO COELHO

What are you most grateful for today? List 5 things that first come to mind this morning:

What do you want to accomplish today? What's important for you to finish by the end of the day? What can you do today to get you one step closer to your goal?

What are your top desires that you would like the universe to work on today?

What is your life going to look like 5 years from now? Write it in the present tense as if it's already been 5 years and you're writing from the future. What have you accomplished? Who have you inspired? Are you fulfilled? How do you feel about the past 5 years of your life?

Set an intention for today:

What is your overall mood this morning? Why do you think that is?

Do you have anything to let go of before you start your day? Journal it out here to let out any frustrations, stresses, worries, or any other negative emotions that won't serve you today

Take a couple of minutes to meditate before you move on with your day. This can be as easy as taking 3-5 deep breaths in silence, or listen to the 5-minute guided meditation download provided. Once done, write down anything that came to mind. Share any inspirations that popped up from the space of stillness:

What is your biggest goal that you created from the goal setting workshop for the next 21 days? Write it down below to keep your subconscious mind focused on it throughout the day:

MORNING MANTRA OF THE *Day*

"My life is entirely and completely up to me. I am a powerful co-creator with the unlimited Universe."

Repeat out loud 5 times with conviction to jumpstart your day with a piece of inspiring truth.

Evening Section:

Rate your day on a scale of 1-10, and explain why you chose the number that you did:

How can you make tomorrow even better?

One thing you can choose to improve upon to keep growing and becoming the best version of yourself:

Did you make any progress today toward your 21-day goal?

Did you accomplish everything you wanted to today? If not, how can you intend to do so tomorrow?

5 things you love and appreciate about yourself:

Let out anything about your day that isn't serving you before bed. This is a safe space to write about any frustrations, worries, doubts or fears so that you can go to bed in peace:

End your day with 3 wishes or desires. What would you like your subconscious mind to work on overnight? Are there any questions you would like answered by the Universe?

SPREAD LOVE EVERYWHERE YOU GO.
LET NO ONE EVER COME TO YOU
WITHOUT LEAVING. *happier*

- MOTHER TERESA

21 Days Are Done. Now What?

Congratulations, beautiful! You have done some pretty damn incredible inner work on yourself over the last 21 days. Now that the journey has come to an end, I want to remind you that it's not really the end, nor will it ever be.

This is a lifetime journey.

Manifesting your kickass life isn't something that just takes place over 21 days. It's something maintained over a lifetime. You now know how to set goals. You know how to set intentions. You have been practicing asking the Universe and your subconscious mind for what you want. You have been practicing major gratitude. You know how to use mantras. You have been inspired by *many* quotes. And, you have been exploring the inner workings of your mind and your soul through transformational journaling prompts.

My biggest recommendation to you is to keep practicing what resonated with you most. Set another goal for the next 21 days using the same formula we used in the beginning of the journal, and rock that new goal too. Track your progress, focus on your three tasks, create your daily to-dos, and most importantly, keep taking massive action in the direction of your dreams.

Manifesting your kickass life is about the small shifts that occur on a daily basis. It's about the daily habits. It's about the small, incremental mindset shifts that happen over time. Personal growth, overcoming anxiety, up leveling, getting to know yourself-- it's not a race. Be gentle with yourself. Have compassion for yourself. Be proud of the work that you have done over the last 21 days and get excited for even more incredible shifts coming your way.

To take this journey to the next level, feel free to invest in a beautiful journal (I am absolutely in love with my Louis Vuitton one), a pen that makes you feel high vibe and amazing, and create a journaling ritual of your own. Remember that your journal is your tool. Whether you are feeling up or down, come back to this incredible tool. Let things out and work through negative emotions on a daily basis. Celebrate each day, focus on what you're grateful for, and create new goals and desires. This is a tool that will serve you for a lifetime. Fall in love with the process and it will fall in love with you.

Cheers to manifesting your kickass life.

To Your Massive Success,

Kathrin Zenkina
Master Mindset Coach
& Success Strategist
Creator of Manifestation Babe

Some Extra Space for you to manifest all of your desires...

ABOUT THE BOOK:

If you've ever felt an itch to discover who you are, what you want out of life, and become the best version of yourself, then you have come to the right place. *She's Killin It* is a 21 day journal to help you manifest your kickass life. Filled with thought provoking prompts, inspirational quotes, motivational mantras, and tons of space to dig deep into the depths of you soul, *She's Killin' It* is a journey unlike any other. In just 21 days you can expect to learn how to set goals effectively, set daily intentions, majorly reduce anxiety levels through therapeutic prompts, form positive habits, and gain crystal clarity of your biggest dreams and desires. Best of all, you'll have fun the entire journey. Expect to grow into the best version of yourself and kill it at this thing called life.

ABOUT THE AUTHOR:

Kathrin Zenkina is a master mindset coach and success strategist for spiritual women and entrepreneurs. She is the creator of the Manifestation Babe brand, a personal development company with a simple yet extremely empowering mission: To empower women to unleash their inner magic, breakthrough their limitations, and manifest realities wilder than their dreams. When Kathrin isn't busy creating inspirational content for the Manifestation Babe tribe on Facebook, Instagram, and manifestationbabe.com, she is traveling the world with her boyfriend, Brennan, and enjoying endless cups of coffee.

ADDITIONAL RESOURCES:

To find out more about manifesting a reality wilder than your dreams and accessing every single freebie resource I've ever put out on Manifestation Babe, access it by visiting manifestationbabe.com/free.

Love VIP treatment? I invite you to check out the only monthly membership you will ever need for all things mindset, manifesting and money. I created an entire personal development hub filled with masterclasses, guided meditations, hypnosis audios, workbooks, eBooks, online business resources, trainings & tools, and so much more that members have lifetime access to. Each month, I add 2-3 new pieces of content to the growing club. Join the VIP MB Tribe at manifestationbabe.com/joinvipmbtribe for just $1.11 per day.

Join over 25,000 babes by joining the Manifestation Babes group on Facebook. I pop into the group and connect with all the beautiful souls inside on a regular basis. I would love to connect with you there! Join us by visiting: https://www.facebook.com/groups/manifestationbabesgroup/

Follow me on Instagram at @ManifestationBabe to stay up to date on even more tips, tricks, and updates on all things mindset, money, journaling and manifesting.

SHE'S **KILLIN'** IT

Made in the USA
Lexington, KY
17 February 2018